IT'S SCIENCE!

Plants and Flowers

Sally Hewitt

W

FRANKLIN WATTS
NEW YORK • LONDON

First published in 1998 by Franklin Watts
96 Leonard Street, London EC2A 4RH

Franklin Watts Australia
14 Mars Road
Lane Cove
NSW 2066

Copyright © Franklin Watts 1998
This edition 1999
Series editor: Rachel Cooke
Designer: Mo Choy
Picture research: Alex Young
Photography: Ray Moller unless otherwise acknowledged
Series consultant: Sally Nankivell-Aston

A CIP catalogue record for this book
is available from the British Library.

ISBN 0 7496 3061 2

Dewey Classification 581.1

Printed in Malaysia

Acknowledgements:
Bruce Coleman Limited pp. 7tr (Charlie Ott), 7tl, 7c, 12c, 26/27c (Hans Reinhard), 10l (Geoff Dore),
12tl, 14ct (Dr Eckart Pott), 12cl, 20br (Jane Burton), 12cr (Sir Jeremy Grayson), 19bl (John Shaw),
20l, 22bl (Kim Taylor), 21br (Felix Labhardt), 24bl (George McCarthy), 25tr (Robert P. Carr)
NHPA: pp. 7bl (David Woodfall), 14c (GI Bernard), 18tr (EA Janes), 19tr, 19c (Stephen Dalton),
22l (Laurie Campbell), 22tr (GJ Cambridge), 24br (Alan Williams)
OSF: pp. 14l (ER Degginger), 14bc, 22c, 23tr (Bob Gibbons), 18tl (Deni Brown), 18tc (Densey Cline),
18bl, 22br, 25l (Gordon Maclean), 21tr (Rob A. Tyrrel), 25bl (Breck P. Kent)
Holt International Studios: p. 23tl (Nigel Catlin).
Thanks to our model, James Moller.

Contents

Using plants

Hundreds of the things you use and eat every day come from plants.

The table mat, the loaf of bread, apples and the table are just some of the things in this picture that come from plants.

Look at the next page to see which plants they come from.

Farmers grow fields of wheat. The **seeds** from the wheat are ground to make flour. We use the flour to make bread.

Wood from tree trunks is used to make furniture.

Apples grow on apple trees.

The table mat is made of cotton. The fluffy cotton bolls that grow on cotton plants are made into cotton thread. The thread is woven together to make cloth.

 THINK ABOUT IT!

Think about the things you use and eat every day. Which of them come from plants?

Growing plants

Plants need sunlight, air, soil and water to grow. A gardener makes sure the plants in the garden get these things so they will grow well.

Today Charlie is watering his plants and digging up **weeds**.

 **THINK ABOUT IT!**

Why do you think Charlie is digging up weeds like this?

TRY IT OUT!

You can grow some plants on cotton wool rather than soil. Try growing mustard in these different ways.

You will need:
- a packet of mustard seeds
- 3 saucers
- a roll of cotton wool
- a cardboard box

Put a layer of cotton wool in each saucer and sprinkle some mustard seeds on top.

1. With one saucer of seeds, dampen the cotton wool with water and leave the seeds in the light. Keep the cotton wool damp over the next 6 days.

2. With another saucer, leave the seeds in the light but don't water them.

3. With the last saucer, dampen the cotton wool and keep it damp but hide the saucer under the box in the dark. Look what happens to the seeds after 6 days.

 THINK ABOUT IT!

Why do you think the seeds in the first saucer grew the best?

9

Making food

Plants and animals need **energy** from food to live and grow. Animals eat plants and other animals for food. Plants don't eat anything. They make their own food.

Plants use energy from sunlight, the air all around them and water from the soil to make food in their green **leaves**.

 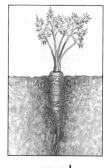 

seed   root   bulb

Plants store the food they need to grow in different places, including the **roots** and **stem**.

Seeds and **bulbs** have a store of food so that new plants can grow before they have leaves to make their own food.

 LOOK AGAIN

Look again at page 9. What happens when a plant is kept out of the sunlight?

Water from the soil travels along the roots, up the stem, and into every part of the plant.

 TRY IT OUT!

Add some food colouring to a glass of water and put in a white carnation. Watch the **flower** slowly turn blue. Why do think this happens?

Blood travels through **veins** in your body. Water travels through veins in leaves.

 **TRY IT OUT!**

Collect some leaves. Feel both sides. Lay some white paper over the rough side of a leaf and rub over it with wax crayon. Watch the pattern of veins appear.

Name the parts

Not all plants grow flowers, but many of them do.
Some flowers are tiny and difficult to see.
Other flowers are big and brightly coloured.

Look at all the different shapes of the
flowers on this page.

TRY IT OUT!

Ask if you can pick some flowers (you will
only need one of each kind) or cut out
pictures of flowers from a catalogue.
Sort the flowers three different ways –
into colours, then into shapes and
then into sizes.

Colour   Shape

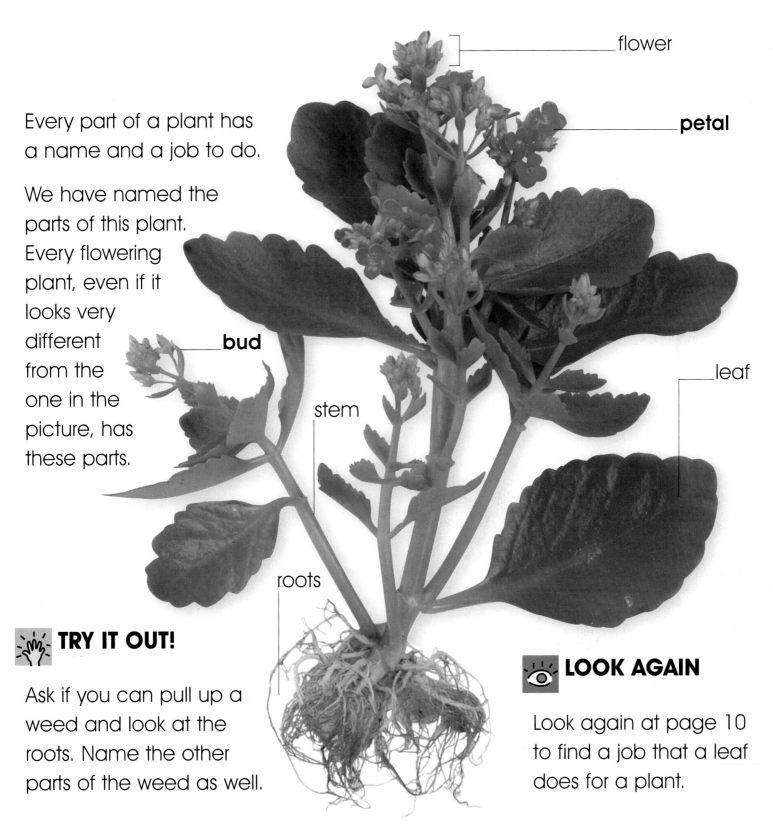

flower

petal

Every part of a plant has a name and a job to do.

We have named the parts of this plant. Every flowering plant, even if it looks very different from the one in the picture, has these parts.

bud

leaf

stem

roots

🖐 **TRY IT OUT!**

Ask if you can pull up a weed and look at the roots. Name the other parts of the weed as well.

👁 **LOOK AGAIN**

Look again at page 10 to find a job that a leaf does for a plant.

13

New plants

Plants start their lives in all kinds of different ways.

A sunflower grows from a seed.

Some new plants grow from tubers under the ground – the potatoes we eat are **tubers**. A new potato plant grows from an old potato.

An onion plant grows from an onion, which is a kind of bulb.

A giant oak tree grows from an acorn. An acorn is a type of seed called a **nut**.

👁 LOOK AGAIN

Look again at page 10. What do seeds, bulbs and nuts store so that new plants can grow?

TRY IT OUT!

Cut the top off a carrot and put it in a saucer of water.

Fill a glass container with water and find an onion that fits into the top. Make sure the bottom of the onion is touching the water.

Collect nuts, **fruit** pips, seeds and stones and plant them in some soil.

Leave them in a place with plenty of light and keep them watered.

Watch out every day for signs that they are growing.

Grow a seed

A bean is a kind of seed. It will grow into a bean plant. New beans that you can pick and eat will grow on the plant.

Beans

☀ THINK ABOUT IT!

If you did not eat the new beans, what could you do with them instead? How could you get even more beans?

✋ TRY IT OUT!

Try growing some beans yourself.
You will need:
- a jar
- cotton wool
- packet of beans.

16

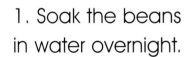

1. Soak the beans in water overnight.

2. Line the jar with cotton wool. Put a little water in the jar so that the cotton wool is damp through.

3. Tuck a few of the soaked beans between the cotton wool and the side of the jar. Keep the cotton wool damp.

 LOOK AGAIN

Look again at page 10. What will the bean plant be able to do once it has grown its green leaves?

4. Watch the root grow downwards, searching for water.

5. Watch the shoot grow upwards, searching for sunlight.

Pollen

Look inside some flowers and you will see a long thin stalk covered in a yellow powder. The stalk is called a **stamen** and the yellow powder is called **pollen**.

Can you see the long stamens covered in pollen in all these different flowers?

 TRY IT OUT!

Brush your finger on to stamens in a flower and see the polllen on your finger. Be careful, pollen can stain your fingers and clothes. Pollen also gives some people **hayfever**.

Flowers use pollen to make their seeds. To do this, pollen has to be carried from one flower to another flower. How can this happen when flowers can't move? Something else does the job for them – flying insects, and sometimes even birds and bats.

A bee lands on this dandelion to drink sweet juice called **nectar**. Pollen rubs off onto the bee's back.

The bee flies off carrying the pollen to a new flower. Now this flower will be able to make seeds for a new plant to grow.

Some plants use the wind to carry pollen. Wind blows sedge pollen from flower to flower.

 THINK ABOUT IT!

Why do you think sedge flowers have to make much more pollen than a dandelion?

19

Come to dinner

Flowers open out in the warm weather when insects are buzzing around looking for food. The flowers can give them this food.

Most flowers make sugary nectar. Other flowers make extra pollen for the insects to eat. Now they must make sure the insects find them.

Flowers have different ways of inviting insects to come to dinner.

Butterflies visit brightly coloured flowers.

Moths cannot see bright colours because they fly at night. They visit flowers with a sweet smell.

👁 LOOK AGAIN

Look again at page 19 to find out why flowers need insects to visit them.

An iris has guide-lines that show insects where to land to find nectar.

Hummingbirds have long beaks to reach for nectar inside brightly coloured flowers.

These orchids trick male insects into visiting them by looking just like a female insect!

TRY IT OUT!

Watch flowers on a sunny day and look out for all the different visitors.

21

Fruits and seeds

When colourful petals have done their job, they die and fall off the flower. Now you can see the fruit forming. The fruit contains the seeds.

Rose petals die leaving a bright red rose hip. The hip is the fruit. It is full of seeds.

Sunflower heads are packed with stripy seeds.

There are thistle seeds inside tiny fruits at the end of each of these fluffy parachutes.

When the orange blossom petals die, tiny oranges start to grow. Pips inside the orange are seeds.

New chestnut trees grow from shiny nuts.

 TRY IT OUT!

Ask an adult to help you to cut open fruit from your fruit bowl. Find the pips, seeds and stones inside the fruit. Can you spot the seeds in all these fruits?

Spreading seeds

When you buy a packet of seeds, you plant the seeds carefully and make sure they have water and sunlight. Seeds of wild plants have to do this job for themselves.

Fruit and nuts are good to eat and this can be a good thing for the plant, too.

Birds eat **berries** and the seeds fall on to the ground in their droppings.

Squirrels bury a store of nuts for the winter and often forget where they are. The birds and squirrels have planted the seeds!

Look at all these other ways
that seeds get spread about.

Cranesbill seed pods burst open
when they are touched and the
seeds shoot out.

Maple seeds
whirl away
from the tree
on wings.

Little hooks on
burrs catch
onto the fur of
a passing
animal and are
carried away.

 LOOK AGAIN

Look again at page 22 to find
some seeds that are a good
shape to be blown along by
the wind.

25

Starting again

Start anywhere on the circle and follow it round to see how poppies start a new life each year.

In the summer, insects visit the bright red flowers. They take pollen from one flower to the next.

In the spring, rain falls, the weather gets warmer and the seed starts to grow into a new plant.

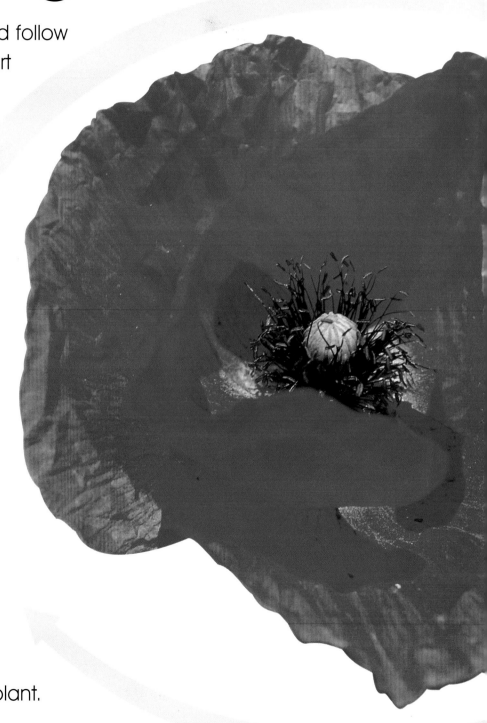

The petals drop off and a head full of seeds is left behind. Wind blows the seed head and seeds shake on to the ground.

Earth and leaves cover the seeds in the autumn. The seeds lie under the earth during the cold winter.

TRY IT OUT!

Plant a bulb (for example, a hyacinth, tulip or daffodil) in a pot in the autumn. Put the bulb somewhere cool and dark for the winter and be very patient! In the spring, put the bulb somewhere warm and light and watch it grow.

Useful words

Berry Berries such as strawberries and blueberries are small juicy fruits with seeds inside them.

Bud New flowers or leaves that are ready to grow are tightly contained inside a bud.

Bulb A bulb is like a bud that grows underground. It is full of food that the new plant needs to grow.

Energy Plants, people and animals all need energy to grow. They get this energy from food. Plants use energy from the sun to make the food they need grow.

Flower Flowers come in all shapes, sizes and colours. They are the parts of a plant where seeds are formed. New plants will grow from the seeds.

Fruit Fruit contains the seeds of the plant. A cherry is the fruit of a cherry tree, the stone in its middle is the seed.

Hayfever When some people breathe in pollen, it makes them sneeze and may give them sore eyes and throat. If this happens, we say they have an allergy called hayfever.

Leaf A leaf is part of a plant. The green colour in a plant's leaves catches the sunlight it needs to make its own food.

Nectar Flowering plants make a sugary liquid food called nectar to attract birds and insects. The animals take pollen from flower to flower, when they feed on the nectar.

Nut A nut is a kind of fruit with a seed inside it protected by a hard shell.

Petal Petals are part of a flower. They protect the stamen. They often have bright colours to attract insects.

Pollen Pollen is the yellow dust flowers use to make their seeds. Pollen has to be moved from one flower to another before a seed can form.

Root A root is the part of a plant that reaches down into the soil to collect the water a plant needs to grow. Roots hold the plant firm in the ground.

Seed A plant grows from a seed. A seed contains a new plant and store of food so that it can begin to grow. The outercase of the seed protects the new plant.

Stamen A stamen is the part of a flower that makes pollen. It is the thin stalk covered in pollen you see in the middle of some flowers.

Stem A stem is part of a plant that is usually fairly long and thin. Roots grow from the bottom of the stem into the ground, leaves and flowers grow on the stem above the ground.

Tubers A tuber is a swollen stem that grows underground. It is full of food the plant needs to grow.

Veins You can see the veins in leaves. Veins are thin tubes that carry water through a plant.

Weed Gardeners and farmers call plants that grow where they don't want them to grow weeds.

Index

About this book

Children are natural scientists. They learn by touching and feeling, noticing, asking questions and trying things out for themselves. The books in the *It's Science!* series are designed for the way children learn. Familiar objects are used as starting points for further learning. *Plants and flowers* starts with food on a table and explores plants and how they grow.

Each double page spread introduces a new topic, such as fruit and seeds. Information is given, questions asked and activities suggested that encourage children to make discoveries and develop new ideas for themselves. Look out for these panels throughout the book:

TRY IT OUT! indicates a simple activity, using safe materials, that proves or explores a point.
THINK ABOUT IT! indicates a question inspired by the information on the page but which points the reader to areas not covered by the book.
LOOK AGAIN introduces a cross-referencing activity which links themes and facts through the book.

Encourage children not to take the familiar world for granted. Point things out, ask questions and enjoy making scientific discoveries together.